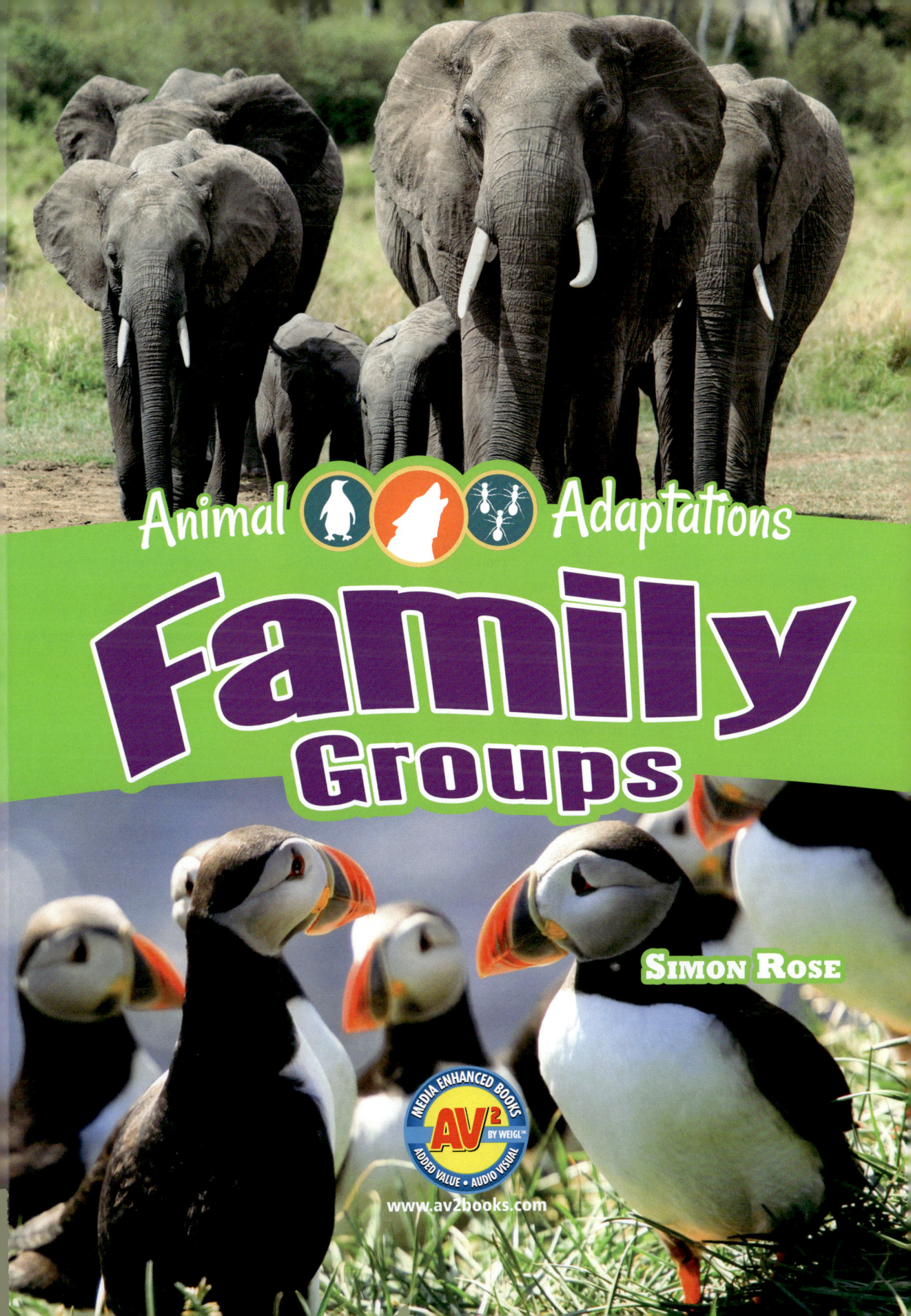

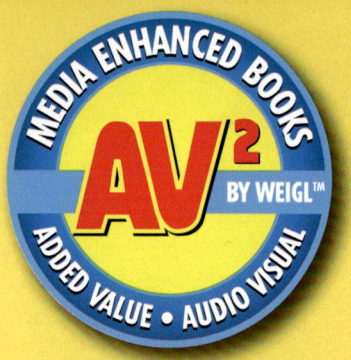

AV² provides enriched content that supplements and complements this book. Weigl's AV² books strive to create inspired learning and engage young minds in a total learning experience.

Your AV² Media Enhanced books come alive with...

 **Audio** Listen to sections of the book read aloud.

 **Key Words** Study vocabulary, and complete a matching word activity.

Go to www.av2books.com, and enter this book's unique code.

 **Video** Watch informative video clips.

 **Quizzes** Test your knowledge.

BOOK CODE

A982894

 **Embedded Weblinks** Gain additional information for research.

 **Slide Show** View images and captions, and prepare a presentation.

AV² by Weigl brings you media enhanced books that support active learning.

 **Try This!** Complete activities and hands-on experiments.

... and much, much more!

Published by AV² by Weigl
350 5th Avenue, 59th Floor
New York, NY 10118
Website: www.av2books.com

Copyright ©2016 AV² by Weigl
All rights reserved. No part of this publication may be reproduced, stored in a retrieval system, or transmitted in any form or by any means, electronic, mechanical, photocopying, recording, or otherwise, without the prior written permission of the publisher.

Library of Congress Cataloging-in-Publication Data

Rose, Simon, 1961- author.
 Family groups / Simon Rose.
   pages cm. -- (Animal adaptations)
 Includes index.
 ISBN 978-1-4896-3667-6 (hard cover : alk. paper) -- ISBN 978-1-4896-3668-3 (soft cover : alk. paper) -- ISBN 978-1-4896-3669-0 (single user ebook) -- ISBN 978-1-4896-3670-6 (multi-user ebook)
 1. Familial behavior in animals--Juvenile literature. 2. Animal behavior--Juvenile literature. 3. Adaptation (Biology)--Juvenile literature. I. Title. II. Series: Animal adaptations (AV2 by Weigl)
 QL761.5.R67 2016
 591.56'3--dc23
                           2015000828

Printed in the United States of America in Brainerd, Minnesota
1 2 3 4 5 6 7 8 9   19 18 17 16 15

052015
WEP051515

Project Coordinator Aaron Carr
Art Director Terry Paulhus

Every reasonable effort has been made to trace ownership and to obtain permission to reprint copyright material. The publishers would be pleased to have any errors or omissions brought to their attention so that they may be corrected in subsequent printings.

Photo Credits
Weigl acknowledges Getty Images as its primary photo supplier for this title.

Contents

AV² Book Code 2

What Is an Adaptation? 4

What Are Family Groups? 6

How Do Animals
Use Family Groups? 8

Types of Family Groups 10

How Does It Work? 12

Timeline 14

Human Family Groups 16

Family Groups
and Biodiversity 18

Conservation 20

Activity 21

Quiz 22

Key Words/Index 23

Log on to www.av2books.com 24

What Is an Adaptation?

For most animals living in the wild, life is a constant battle to survive. Many animals have developed features that help them to survive in their natural **habitat**. These features are known as adaptations. There are a number of reasons for animal adaptations. These include survival in extreme heat and cold, finding food and water, and avoiding **predators**. Animals adapt over thousands or even millions of years. If an adaptation is successful, it is likely that parents will pass it on to their young. The successful adaptation will help the **species** survive. This process is called **natural selection**.

One way in which animals can increase their chances of survival is to be part of a group. Living in a group is a type of adaptation. Animals that live in groups are more likely to survive than those that live alone. Being part of a group can make life safer for young animals.

All adults in a wolf family group care for the young.

5 AMAZING ADAPTATIONS

These animals have adapted to live in family groups.

Capybaras

Capybaras live in family groups of between 10 and 20 animals, called herds. A herd has one **dominant** male, several females, their young, and a few other males. The other males watch out for predators.

Zebras

Zebras spend much of their time traveling to find food. They graze and sleep together in large family groups, called herds. When danger threatens a herd with young zebras, called colts, the herd forms a protective ring around the mothers and colts.

Gorillas

Gorillas live in groups of 6 to 12, called a troop. Adult males are called silverbacks. A troop is made up of an adult male, a group of females, and their young. Young males leave to live by themselves or form a new troop.

Prairie dogs

Prairie dogs live in family groups called coteries. They live in connecting tunnels. These tunnels have separate areas for sleeping, caring for young animals, and storing food.

Orcas

Orcas live in family groups of up to 40 members. These groups are called pods. A pod includes the orca mother and her young. All the members of the pod are related.

Animal Adaptations

What Are Family Groups?

Family groups are animals of the same species that live together. These groups may be very small, with just a few animals, or huge, with thousands of animals. Some are complex groups, where every animal has a special role. Others are loose groups that form only at certain times of year or for a particular reason, such as when traveling between summer and winter habitats.

HERDS

Large, plant-eating **mammals**, such as elephants, wildebeests, and bison, form herds. A herd can be a small group of related animals. Sometimes, herds join together to form a larger group. During migration, a herd can have thousands of animals.

COLONIES

Some birds, bats, tortoises, and insects form colonies. These are very large groups of the same species of animal. Some colonies form only at certain times of the year. For many seabirds, such as gannets, this includes the nesting season.

EUSOCIAL SPECIES

Eusocial species live in very organized social groups. These species include ants, bees, termites, and wasps. The **queen** and her **mate** are the only members of the colony that **breed**. The others gather food, protect the colony, and raise the young. In a eusocial group, all the members of the colony depend on one another.

ELEPHANT FAMILIES

Female elephants live in small family groups with their young. The head of the herd is called the matriarch. The herd is made up of the matriarch, her sisters, and their **offspring**. Young males stay with their mother's herd until they are adults. Then they either live alone or form a group with other males.

The Matriarch

The matriarch is usually the oldest female. She is very important because she has gained experience of how to survive. She makes the important decisions, such as when and where the herd should eat.

The Herd

An elephant herd has between 6 and 12 members. The females all work together to look after the young and protect each other.

Calves

A female elephant has a calf every four or five years. A newborn calf weighs about 220 pounds (100 kilograms). Female calves spend their whole lives with their mother's herd. Males stay for 10 to 14 years.

Animal Adaptations

How Do Animals Use Family Groups?

Being part of a group can provide protection and support. It can make getting food easier. Some animals that live in groups hunt **prey** together. Others help each other find food. Some animal groups work together to protect themselves against predators. In some groups, the animals work together to care for their young.

Caring for Young
In a group of lions, called a pride, the females all have cubs at around the same time. Female lions often feed one another's cubs. They protect the cubs from adult males that might attack them.

Hunting and Finding Food
Wolves and other animals, such as coyotes and hyenas, hunt in packs. This means that they can help each other bring down larger animals. The members of the pack then share the food.

Protection against Predators
A group of meerkats is called a clan. One or two meerkats act as lookouts while the others search for food. If a lookout spots a predator, it gives a warning cry. The meerkats then escape to safety in their underground burrows.

Meerkats have two different alarm calls. One is for a land-based predator and the other is for an air-based predator, such as a bird.

Wolf Packs in the Food Chain

A family group of wolves is called a pack. A pack is led by a pair of wolves, one dominant male and one dominant female. These are the only wolves in the pack that breed. Wolves are **tertiary consumers**. They eat other animals. Wolves have adapted to living in family groups to increase the chances of success when hunting prey. Badgers have also adapted to living together, in underground burrows. This helps to protect them from predators such as wolves. Badgers are **secondary consumers**. They eat insects, small mammals, and birds. Grasshoppers are **primary consumers**. They eat plants, called producers, which receive their energy from the Sun.

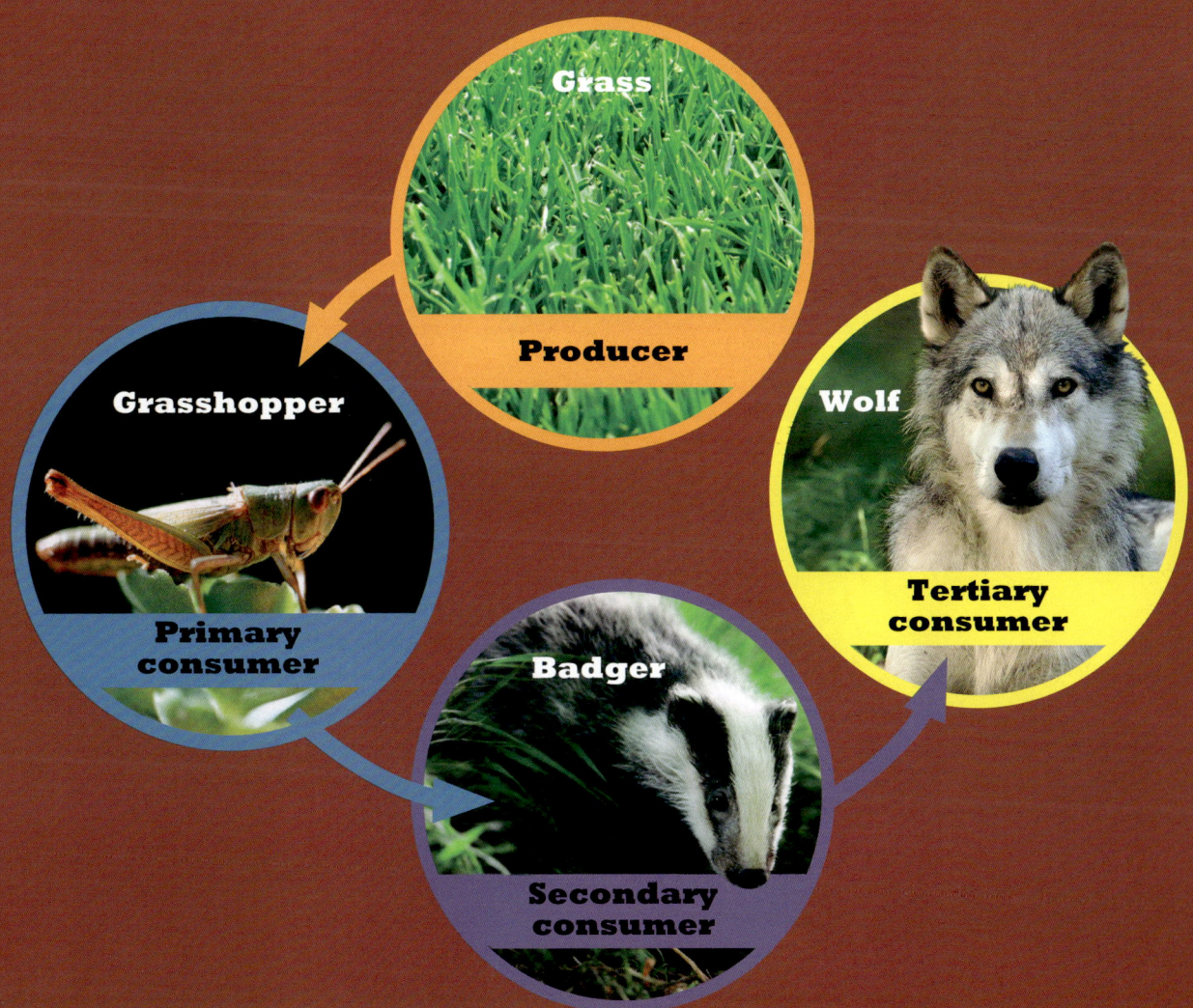

Types of Family Groups

There are many types of animal family groups. Some animal family groups, such as penguins, have a male, a female, and their young. Some have one male and a number of females and their young. The male defends these females from other males. In some species, the males only join the group for the breeding season. In these families, the family group is made up of females and their young. Sometimes, small families join with other animals to form large herds.

The way animals in a family group behave varies as much as the types of families. In meerkat families, the older offspring help to raise the younger ones. In emperor penguin families, the males sit on the eggs. In lion families, the females do the hunting. In eusocial colonies, several generations live and work together.

Two types of mole rats are the only mammals that live in eusocial colonies. All other eusocial animals are insects.

4 TYPES OF FAMILY GROUPS

Nuclear Family

Beavers live in small family groups, called nuclear families. The family group is made up of two parents, a male and a female, and their offspring. Beavers stay with the same mate for life.

Extended Family

A zebra family has a **stallion**, several **mares**, and their young. There are 5 to 20 zebras in a family. A family will often join other families to form a herd. However, members of each family still stay close to one another within the herd.

Loose Family Group

Atlantic puffins form large breeding colonies each spring and summer. They land on sea coasts and islands in the North Atlantic region. Puffin nests are usually built on rocky cliff tops.

Complex Family

Termite colonies can have millions of individuals. They are very organized and have three main **castes**. These are workers, soldiers, and the termites that reproduce.

Animal Adaptations 11

How Does It Work?

Being part of a family group has advantages other than care of the young, protection, and help in getting food. Saving energy is important for animals. Eusocial colonies are very efficient because there are thousands of animals, each with its own role.

Being in a family group gives animals a better chance of defending the resources of their habitat, such as food. Huddling together can keep animals warm enough to survive winter. When animals **migrate** in a group, there are more eyes to watch for predators. Migrating birds find their way better by traveling in a flock. This is because birds that have migrated before have knowledge of the journey. Animals in large colonies have a greater chance of finding a mate.

In a pride of lions, the females do the hunting.

4 WAYS ANIMALS LIVE IN FAMILY GROUPS

Colonies of Penguins

Emperor penguins huddle together in groups of up to 6,000 to keep warm in the cold Antarctic climate. The penguins on the outside gradually move into the middle. This means that every penguin gets a chance to be in the warm center.

Pods of Whales

Beluga whale pods have males and females. In calving season, some pods only have mothers and their young. The average pod has about 10 members. Beluga pods sometimes join together for migrations. These large groups have between 200 and 10,000 belugas.

Troops of Gorillas

The leader of a gorilla troop is the largest, oldest silverback. He makes all the decisions. He decides when the troop looks for food, eats, moves elsewhere, and sleeps. He protects the troop and becomes **aggressive** if he thinks the troop is threatened.

Eusocial Colonies of Ants

Ant colonies have three main castes that work together. The queen's job is to lay eggs so that the colony can survive. Worker ants are all females. They care for the queen and her young. Workers build and repair nests, search for food, and defend the colony against enemies. Male ants do not work and die soon after mating with queens.

Animal Adaptations

Timeline

Earth has changed in many ways over the course of millions of years. Some species have adapted to these changes and have survived. Other species have not been able to adapt and have become **extinct**. Ants have lived on Earth since the time of the dinosaurs. Over millions of years, ants have adapted to living in almost every part of the world. Today, they are found almost everywhere in the world except Antarctica. An ant colony is a very busy and crowded place.

An ant colony depends on its workers to take care of the young.

Ant Explosion

300 million years ago

Nearly all of Earth's land is joined up in a single landmass. Over hundreds of millions of years, as Earth's plates move, the landmass also moves about.

200 million years ago

The huge single landmass begins to split up into separate continents. This causes changes to habitats. Plants and animals adapt to these changes or become extinct.

140 to 168 million years ago

The first ants appear. They are very like wasps. They live in what, today, is called the Northern Hemisphere. There are not many ants in comparison with the number of other insects. There are not many types of ants.

100 million years ago

The first flowering plants appear, giving ants many new food sources. Many different species of ants develop. They live in burrows and leaf litter, or build nests in the treetops. Some species eat seeds, leaves, and fruit. Some species eat other insects.

Today

Ants are the most numerous insects on Earth. There are about 12,500 known ant species. There may be thousands not yet discovered. The combined weight of all the ants is greater than the combined weight of all the mammals, birds, reptiles, and **amphibians**.

Human Family Groups

Life for early people was challenging. They had little or no shelter and few weapons. They competed with the animals for food. These people lived among four-footed predators, such as leopards, that could run much faster than they could on their two feet. They learned that by cooperating with one another, they could defend themselves. They also learned that, to be successful hunters themselves, they needed to work as a group.

Human children take much longer to become independent than young animals. They need more care. They need warmth and shelter. It is hard to protect a child from predators while searching for food. By forming family groups, people were able to share the tasks involved in surviving, such as finding food and shelter and caring for their young.

By working as a team, humans were able to hunt larger animals.

Young animals learn skills by watching the adults. They play games, such as pretending to hunt, to practice these skills. Human children watch adults cook, drive cars, and fix things. Their games often involve pretending to do these things.

Skills such as running and catching may not be as important for human survival today as they were in the past. However, the other skills that sport and games teach are. Humans still need to learn how to work together and get along.

Children gain physical skills by playing games. They also learn how to share and work together.

Family Groups and Biodiversity

Biodiversity refers to the variety of life in a habitat or **biome**. Animals often develop adaptations to fit a specific habitat. Some animals, such as chimpanzees, depend on having a high level of diversity in their habitat. Other animals, such as humpback whales, travel long distances to their feeding grounds.

Female chimpanzees and their offspring have strong bonds, even after the offspring become adults. A male chimpanzee stays in his mother's family group, or troop, all his life. Males also have strong relationships with other males in the troop. Chimpanzees groom each other for cleaning and to keep friendships. Adults teach their young the skills they will use as adults. These include how to use tools, make nests, and climb trees. The territory of a chimpanzee troop can vary from a few square miles to hundreds of square miles. Loss of habitat is causing a drop in the number of chimpanzees.

A young chimpanzee rides on its mother's back until it is about two years old.

Humpback whales sometimes travel in loose groups of about 15 whales. In summer, they feed close to the polar regions. Every year, they migrate from their feeding grounds to warmer waters near the equator. This is where the whales find mates and have their offspring. When a calf is born, its mother helps it to the surface. The bond between a female and her calf is very strong. They swim close together. They often touch each other's flippers as a sign of affection.

Humpback calves stay close to their mothers until they are about a year old.

Conservation

Many animals are suited to living together in a certain environment. If the environment changes, the animals could become extinct. Human activity threatens many areas where animals live in groups and colonies.

In some places, wolves have been killed because they are believed to attack livestock. Elsewhere, roads have been made on land that migrating animals cross. Pollution is killing colonies of bees. In some parts of Africa where gorillas and chimpanzees live, people are building roads and logging trees. This threatens these **primates** for two reasons. They lose their forest habitat, and the roads make it easier for poachers to hunt them.

Around the world, people are trying to save the biodiversity of Earth. Wildlife groups work with governments and industry to preserve habitats. **Volunteers** take action to protect endangered animals.

Red crabs usually live alone, but when the wet season begins they all migrate together to their coastal breeding grounds. People have put up notices to try to protect the crabs.

Family Groups

Activity

Match each animal with its type of family group.

Answers: 1.B 2.C 3.A 4.D

Animal Adaptations 21

Quiz

Complete this quiz to test your knowledge of animal family groups.

1 When did ants first appear on Earth?

A. 140 to 168 million years ago

2 Where do puffins build their nests?

A. Rocky cliff tops

3 What are eusocial species?

A. Species that live in very organized social groups

4 What are large adult male gorillas called?

A. Silverbacks

5 What are groups of lions called?

A. Prides

6 What is biodiversity?

A. The variety of life in a particular habitat or biome

7 What is a coterie?

A. A group of prairie dogs

8 What are groups of orcas called?

A. Pods

9 What name is given to the leader of a female elephant herd?

A. Matriarch

10 What are colonies?

A. Large groups of the same kind of animals that live close to each other

Family Groups

Key Words

aggressive: angry and ready to fight

amphibians: animals that live both on land and in the water

biome: a large community of plants and animals that live in a major habitat, such as a forest

breed: have offspring

castes: types of insects in a colony, based on the work they do

dominant: most important, most powerful

extinct: when all members of a species die out

habitat: the natural environment of a living thing

mammals: warm-blooded animals that feed milk to their young and are usually covered with hair or fur

mares: females of any species of horse

mate: a breeding partner

migrate: seasonal movement of animals from one region to another

natural selection: a process whereby animals that have better adapted to their environment survive and pass on those adaptations to their young

offspring: the young of animals

predators: animals that hunt and eat other animals

prey: an animal that is hunted and eaten by another animal

primary consumers: animals that eat plants

primates: mammals such as gorillas and chimpanzees

queen: a reproducing female ant, bee, termite, or wasp

secondary consumers: animals that eat plant-eating animals

species: a group of plants or animals that are alike in many ways

stallion: the male of any species of horse

tertiary consumers: animals that eat other animals

volunteers: people who work without being paid

Index

Africa 20
amphibians 15
Antarctica 14
ants 6, 13, 14, 15, 22

badgers 9
bats 6
beavers 11
bees 6, 20
biomes 18, 22
birds 6, 8, 9, 12, 15
bison 6

capybaras 5
castes 11, 13
chimpanzees 18, 20
clans 8
colonies 6, 10, 11, 12, 13, 14, 20, 21, 22
coteries 5, 22
coyotes 8

crabs 20

elephants 6, 7, 21, 22

gorillas 5, 13, 20, 21, 22
grasshoppers 9

habitats 4, 12, 15, 18, 20, 22
herds 5, 6, 7, 10, 11, 21, 22
hyenas 8

insects 6, 9, 10, 15

leopards 16
lions 8, 10, 12, 22

mammals 6, 9, 10, 15
meerkats 8, 10
mole rats 10

orcas 5, 22

packs 8, 9, 21
penguins 10, 13
pods 5, 13, 22
prairie dogs 5, 22
predators 4, 5, 8, 9, 12, 16
prey 8, 9
prides 8, 12, 22
puffins 11, 22

reptiles 15

termites 6, 11, 21
tortoises 6
troops 5, 13, 18

wasps 6, 15
whales 13, 18, 19
wildebeest 6
wolves 4, 8, 9, 20, 21

zebras 5, 11

Animal Adaptations 23

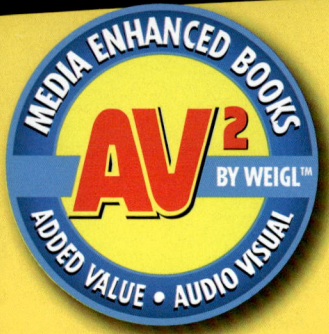

Log on to www.av2books.com

AV² by Weigl brings you media enhanced books that support active learning. Go to www.av2books.com, and enter the special code found on page 2 of this book. You will gain access to enriched and enhanced content that supplements and complements this book. Content includes video, audio, weblinks, quizzes, a slide show, and activities.

AV² Online Navigation

Audio
Listen to sections of the book read aloud.

Book Pages
AV² pages directly correspond to pages in the book.

Video
Watch informative video clips.

Key Words
Study vocabulary, and complete a matching word activity.

Embedded Weblinks
Gain additional information for research.

Try This!
Complete activities and hands-on experiments.

Quizzes
Test your knowledge.

Slide Show
View images and captions, and prepare a presentation.

AV² was built to bridge the gap between print and digital. We encourage you to tell us what you like and what you want to see in the future.

Sign up to be an AV² Ambassador at www.av2books.com/ambassador.

Due to the dynamic nature of the internet, some of the URLs and activities provided as part of AV² by Weigl may have changed or ceased to exist. AV² by Weigl accepts no responsibility for any such changes. All media enhanced books are regularly monitored to update addresses and sites in a timely manner. Contact AV² by Weigl at 1-866-649-3445 or av2books@weigl.com with any questions, comments, or feedback.